Dog Tales:
True Stories About Amazing Dogs

Distinguished Dogs

Dog Tales:
True Stories About Amazing Dogs

Distinguished Dogs
Helping Dogs
Hunting and Herding Dogs
Police Dogs
Search and Rescue Dogs

Dog Tales:
True Stories About Amazing Dogs

Distinguished Dogs

Marie-Therese Miller

CHELSEA
CLUBHOUSE
An Imprint of Chelsea House Publishers

Distinguished Dogs

Chelsea Clubhouse
An imprint of Infobase Publishing
132 West 31st Street
New York, NY 10001

ISBN-10: 0-7910-9039-6
ISBN-13: 978-0-7910-9039-8

Library of Congress Cataloging-in-Publication Data
Miller, Marie-Therese.
    Distinguished dogs / Marie-Therese Miller.
        p. cm. — (Dog tales, true stories about amazing dogs)
    Includes bibliographical references and index.
    ISBN 0-7910-9039-6 (hardcover)
    1. Dogs—Anecdotes—Juvenile literature. I. Title. II. Series.
    SF426.2.M55 2007
    636.7'0886—dc22   2006024085

Chelsea House and Chelsea Clubhouse books are available at special discounts when purchased in bulk quantities for businesses, associations, institutions, or sales promotions. Please call our Special Sales Department in New York at (212) 967-8800 or (800) 322-8755.

You can find Chelsea House and Chelsea Clubhouse on the World Wide Web at http://www.chelseahouse.com

Development Editor: Anna Prokos
Text Designer: Annie O'Donnell
Cover Designer: Ben Peterson

Printed in the United States of America

Bang FOF 10 9 8 7 6 5 4 3 2 1

This book is printed on acid-free paper.

Contents

Sirius's Mission

At 8:46 a.m. on September 11, 2001, Port Authority Police Officer David Lim was in his office in the basement of the World Trade Center's (WTC) south tower. His muscular Labrador retriever, Sirius, was with him. They heard a massive explosion. Officer Lim turned to Sirius and said, "One got by us." He thought a terrorist had bombed the building and that he and his canine partner, who had been trained to sniff for explosives, had not detected the bomb that shook the building.

In 1993, before Sirius was even born, terrorists planted a bomb in a rental truck and parked it in an underground garage of the World Trade Center. That explosion killed six people and injured more than 1,000. Officer Lim and Sirius worked long days to make sure nothing like that happened again.

But it wasn't a bomb that struck the building on September 11. The noise Officer Lim and Sirius had heard was the sound of hijacked airplane American Airlines flight 11 crashing into the north tower of the World Trade Center. Terrorists had flown the plane into the world-famous building, hitting floors 93 through 98.

SIRIUS'S TRAINING

Port Authority Police Officer David Lim first met Sirius at a breeder's home in Pennsylvania. The breeder had been training Sirius to become a hunting dog. He was being taught to retrieve birds from the water, but Sirius didn't want to follow this career path—he refused to set one paw into the water!

Officer Lim believed Sirius could be a fine explosive detection dog, and he made Sirius his canine partner. For 3½ months, the pair attended detector school at Port Newark K-9 Training Center in New Jersey. Sirius learned how to use his keen sense of smell to detect the scent of explosives. During training, Sirius learned to recognize 14 different explosive substances.

When Officer Lim and Sirius graduated from detector training on July 4, 2000, they were assigned the job of keeping the people who

Officer Lim knew that people in the building would need his help, and he knew he couldn't manage his dog and rescue people at the same time. He secured Sirius in his cage while he set off to help others. "Stay right there," he told his K-9 partner. "I'll be back for you."

Officer Lim raced to the WTC north tower and began the long climb up the stairs. He helped injured people get to rescue personnel, and he encouraged fearful masses of people to keep moving down the stairs. When Officer Lim reached the 44th floor at 9:02 a.m., another hijacked airplane, United Airlines flight 175, hit the south tower. Floors 78

worked at and visited the World Trade Center (WTC) in New York City safe.

Each day, Officer Lim and 4-year-old Sirius searched hundreds of vehicles at the WTC for explosives. If a bag or suitcase was left unattended, Sirius would sniff it to determine if it contained a bomb. When world leaders were expected at the WTC, the K-9 team would thoroughly check the area to be certain it was explosive-free.

When Sirius located the explosives' scents, he would sit. This is called a passive alert. Explosive detection dogs do not bark or scratch when they find bombs because that might trigger an explosion. Thanks to Officer Lim, Sirius had learned all he needed to know to perform his brave work as an explosive detection dog.

through 84 were in flames as Sirius waited in that building's basement.

The impact of the airplane flying into the south tower, coupled with the searing heat of the burning jet fuel, weakened the building's internal structure. At 10 a.m., the entire south tower collapsed to the ground.

Meanwhile, Officer Lim was making his way back down the north tower's stairway. As he passed each level, he gathered the physically challenged and elderly people. He made sure nobody was left behind. Officer Lim reached the fourth story when all the floors above him collapsed. Thousands of people were killed and buried in the rubble. Miraculously, though, Officer Lim survived. He was rescued by firefighters five hours later.

Following his rescue, Officer Lim tried desperately to enter the south tower and find Sirius. Fire and police personnel wouldn't let him pass because the unstable remains of the building were just too dangerous.

The Port Authority Police Department lost 37 officers and K-9 Sirius on that fateful day in history. Sirius was the only police dog killed in the terrorist attacks at the World Trade Center.

During the WTC victim recovery, whenever the body of a police officer was discovered, his partner was called to the WTC site. More than four months

PROTECTING THE CITY HUBS

The Port Authority Police Department of New York and New Jersey has 33 K-9 units. Twenty-five of the K-9s are explosive detection dogs, like Sirius and Sprig (Officer Lim's new canine partner), and 8 are narcotics detection dogs that can locate illegal drugs. The officers and their dogs undergo 400 hours of specialized K-9 training.

After training, the Port Authority K-9 units protect many of the transportation centers of New York City and New Jersey. They patrol the area's three major airports, John F. Kennedy International, LaGuardia, and Newark Liberty International. The canine and human teams also keep watch over area bridges, such as the George Washington Bridge, and tunnels, like the Lincoln Tunnel and Holland Tunnel, which are all major gateways into the bustling city. The Port Authority police also keep ships at the Marine Terminal, PATH trains, and Port Authority buses secure.

Port Authority K-9 units protect many of the transportation centers of New York and New Jersey, including the area's three major airports.

after the attacks, on January 22, 2002, Sirius's body was recovered from the rubble. Officer Lim arrived at the site to watch search and rescue personnel drape Sirius's body in an American flag. All the people at the WTC site were silent and the machinery was quieted while Sirius's remains were removed. This silence was one of the ways the rescuers showed their respect for the human dead, and Sirius was afforded the same honor.

"He waited," Officer Lim said of Sirius, "and I came back."

A HERO REMEMBERED

A memorial service for Sirius was held on April 24, 2002, at Liberty State Park in Jersey City, New Jersey. One hundred police officers and their K-9s from all over the United States attended. Bag pipers played the hymn "Amazing Grace," and Sirius was given a 21-gun salute. Office Lim wept when he was presented with Sirius's metal water bowl, which had been recovered from the officer's crushed car. The engraved bowl read: "I gave my life so that you may save others."

Many civilians reached out to offer tribute to the brave dog. A teacher from Illinois dedicated a poem to Sirius, and an artist from Missouri crafted an oil painting of the dog. School children collected money and purchased an oak display case in which Officer Lim could keep the flag that covered Sirius's body.

Port Authority Police Officer David Lim stands between a memorial painting of Sirius, his canine partner who lost his life on September 11, 2001, and his current K-9 partner, Sprig. Sprig is carrying on Sirius's important work.

Like Sirius and Sprig, many dogs work with the Port Authority of New York and New Jersey to keep the busy metropolitan area safe.

Students in Erie, Pennsylvania, heard about Sirius's death. The children wanted to buy Officer Lim another police dog. They held bake sales and car washes to raise funds. The students contacted a breeder in California and told him they wished to purchase a canine for explosive detection work. When the breeder discovered to whom the dog would go, he told the children to keep their money. He donated a black Labrador retriever, named Sprig, to Officer Lim.

Officer Lim says Sprig is an active and wonderful bomb detection dog. The K-9 can check an entire room for explosives in just five minutes. The police pair has searched for bombs at New York City's major tunnels, airports, and the Port Authority bus terminal. Recently, Officer Lim became a trainer at the Port Newark K-9 Training Center, where Sirius was trained. There, Sprig demonstrates to K-9s and their handlers the proper way to find explosives. Officer Lim and Sprig are teaching new heroes how to keep people safe.

A Life-Saving Race

In late 1924, children were dying in Nome, Alaska.
Dr. Curtis Welch, Nome's only physician, examined a 2-year-old Eskimo boy. The doctor noticed that the toddler was very ill and was refusing to eat. The child died the following day, and shortly after, more children with similar symptoms also passed away. By January 1925, Dr. Welch was certain that he was facing a **diphtheria** outbreak.

Diphtheria is a disease caused by bacteria. The symptoms include a sore throat, swollen glands, fever, and weakness. The diphtheria bacteria releases a poison into the body that causes a thick, grayish covering to grow at the back of the throat. The covering can result in breathing trouble. As the toxin moves through the body, it can affect major organs, such as the heart and kidneys.

Diphtheria is highly contagious and can be spread through a simple sneeze or cough. Children are especially vulnerable to the disease. Today, they receive vaccinations to prevent diphtheria, but in the 1920s, an **antitoxin** was the only way to stop the disease's poison from traveling through the body. Without the antitoxin, more children would surely die in Nome and surrounding areas.

Dr. Welch's supply of diphtheria antitoxin was low and the medication was old. He needed a fresh supply of the antitoxin **serum**. But there was a problem: transporting the antitoxin serum to Nome, in the middle of winter, was a serious challenge. The city of Nome is in the northwestern portion of Alaska, only about 142 miles (228.5 km) south of the Arctic Circle. Nome winters are bitterly cold, and the body of water nearest the city, Norton Bay, ices over. No ships can enter or leave. For the duration of the freeze in 1925, Nome was nearly cut off from the rest of the world.

The serum could be shipped to the town of Seward in southeast Alaska. From there, it could be taken by train to Nenana, which was a long, snowy 674 miles

(1,084.7 km) away from Nome. How would the serum get from Nenana to Nome in time to save lives?

In that part of Alaska, dog sleds were often used in the winter to carry goods, including the mail. Nome officials decided to have dog sled teams transport the serum from Nenana to Nome. Each dog sled team would travel a portion of the distance and then pass the serum to the next team.

TEAMING UP

One of the 20 chosen dog sled drivers, also known as a **musher**, was Leonard Seppala. He was a well-respected musher who had won many dog sled races in Alaska. He also worked as a dog sled driver for Hammon Consolidated Gold Fields, a mining company. His fellow worker at Hammon, Gunnar Kaasen, would participate in the serum race, as well.

During that time, dog sled drivers used wooden sleds. They would stand on the rear of the sled as dogs in harnesses pulled it. Most times, the dogs were placed in rows of two across, and as many as 20 dogs might have been used to haul a sled. Strong dogs nearest the sled were called the wheel dogs. The dog in the front was known as the lead dog.

The dogs worked hard for the driver, and the musher treated them well in return. At the end of each trail, the musher checked the dogs' paws for injuries. If they were hurt, the musher administered any needed

Respected musher, Leonard Seppala, stands with his dog team that helped in the race to carry the serum to Nome, Alaska. Togo *(far left)* led the dog sled team for 91 miles, the longest portion of the run.

first aid. He made certain that the canines had plenty of water, and he fed them foods rich in protein, like fish or meat.

The sled dogs needed to have speed, strength, and endurance. The lead dog possessed these qualities, in addition to intelligence and confidence. Lead dogs had to be self-assured enough to help the team travel through blizzards and across icy bodies of water. It had to lead them in below zero temperatures. Because winter days in Alaska can be as short as 4 hours, the lead dog often navigated the trails in the dark.

Leonard Seppala's lead dog was named Togo. He was a 12-year-old male Siberian husky. Gunnar Kaasen also chose a Siberian husky to lead his team. His black dog was named Balto.

Siberian huskies make fine sled dogs. They are fast and energetic. The dogs have a double coat of fur to keep them warm in cold conditions. The breed's eyes are almond-shaped, which limits the eyes' exposure to wind and snow. A Siberian husky's paw pads are close together, tough, and well padded, so the ice on the trail is less likely to cut them. When at rest, the dogs use their curly tails to cover non-furry areas of their bodies in order to protect themselves from the frigid temperatures.

When Togo was a puppy, Seppala didn't think he had the potential to be a successful sled dog, despite his Siberian husky blood. He gave Togo to a woman to keep as a pet. But Togo had a mind—and mission—of his own. He leapt through a window in the woman's house and ran right back to Seppala.

Another day, as Seppala set off on a dog sled journey, he left the 8-month-old Togo at home. Togo broke out and traveled through the night until he caught up with Seppala and the other dogs. On that trip, Seppala tried Togo in the lead position, and the dog proved that he could do the job.

RACE TO THE FINISH

The famous serum run began on January 27, 1925, when Bill Shannon placed the 300,000 units of antitoxin on his sled at Nenana. The serum package was wrapped warmly, so it wouldn't freeze in the Alaskan cold. Shannon and his dogs braved temperatures below 40°F (−40°C) to carry the serum 52 miles (83.7 km) to Tolovana. Three of Shannon's dogs died soon after their journey due to exposure to the frigid weather.

Sixteen more dog teams would run the serum before it was handed to Seppala on January 31. Togo led Seppala's dog team on the longest portion of the run—91 miles (146.5 km) from Shaktoolik to Golovin.

At the start of their trip, the temperature was about −30°F (−34.4°C). It was dark, and a strong winds were blowing. Seppala decided to risk the dangerous journey over the icy Norton Sound because it would save one entire day of travel time.

The crossing could be perilous. The ice might crack and the team could fall into the frigid water or be stranded on an ice floe and swept far out into

Gunnar Kaasen and Balto, along with Kaasen's dog sled team, endured intense blizzard conditions to deliver the antitoxin serum to Dr. Welch. Balto led the dog team for 53 miles.

the Bering Sea. Thankfully, Togo's expert leadership brought them safely across.

In possession of the serum, Kaasen joined the race on February 1. Balto led Kaasen's team through a blizzard. At times, Kaasen couldn't see the trail; he trusted Balto to keep them on track. The temperatures were a chilling –28°F (–33.3°C) with 70 mph (112.7 km/h) winds. A mighty gust of wind flipped the sled over and into a snowbank. The serum went flying. In the dark, Kaasen dropped to his knees and searched through the snow for the antitoxin. He felt a wave of relief when he finally located the package.

The blizzard was so intense that Kaasen missed the place where he was to meet the next musher. He continued to the next rendezvous point. When the team arrived at that drop-off point, the driver of the dog sled team was asleep. The driver believed that Kaasen had been warned to wait until the storm was over before transporting the serum. Kaasen did not wish to waste time by waking the man and having him ready his dog team, so the musher and his dog team kept going.

All told, Balto led Kaasen's dog team 53 miles (85.3 km), all the way to the race's final destination. They arrived in Nome bringing the lifesaving diphtheria antitoxin on February 2, 1925. The serum

AFTER THE RUN

Following the 1925 serum run, Gunnar Kaasen and his lead dog, Balto, caught the attention of the United States. A short Hollywood movie was made about the heroic part they played in the antitoxin run. To honor the dog, a statue of Balto was erected in Central Park in New York City.

A bronze statue of Balto stands in Central Park in New York City, commemorating the dog's famous life-saving serum run.

Leonard Seppala understood that Balto deserved praise for navigating a blizzard to reach Nome. However, he was disappointed that Togo did not receive the same attention. After all, Togo had led Seppala's team on the longest leg of the run, 91 miles (146.5 km), and had crossed the dangerous ice of Norton Sound.

Seppala did eventually tour the United States with Togo, and the dog finally received the accolades he was due. Togo died on December 5, 1929.

Meanwhile, Balto and the rest of the dog team made appearances across the United States. Eventually, the dogs were bought by a person who sold tickets to people wanting to see the famous team. The dogs were like a sideshow exhibit, and their new master did not treat them well.

George Kimble, a businessperson from Cleveland, offered to purchase the dog team for $2,000. The people of Cleveland helped raise the money to buy the dogs. Even the city's school children

(continues)

(continued)

contributed coins. Balto and his teammates were brought to the Brookside Zoo in Cleveland, where he lived comfortably until his death on March 14, 1933. Balto had once saved the lives of children, and the children of Cleveland returned the favor.

allowed Dr. Welch to put an end to the diphtheria epidemic. Thanks to the skillful dogs and their brave mushers, the children of Nome were saved.

Newfoundlands: The Lifeguard Dogs

A woman swims out into the ocean, paddling beyond the breaking waves. Suddenly, she is caught in the current and realizes she cannot struggle back to shore. She flails her arms, shouts for help, and begins to slip beneath the water's surface. With the help of a Newfoundland, this drowning and terrified woman could be rescued.

A Newfoundland has the ability to battle waves and currents and swim to a drowning victim. Newfoundlands are known for their lifesaving skills in the water and are often called lifeguard dogs. The Newfoundland breed first appeared around 1000 AD on the island of, not surprisingly, Newfoundland. The island is now part of Canada and is located to the far east of the country.

Throughout history, these large dogs have worked on boats with fishermen. The dogs were an important part of the fishing team. They carried heavy nets filled with fish. The dogs saved crewmembers that fell into the sea and even towed disabled boats to shore.

The remains of the *S.S. Ethie* still stand on the rocks off the coast of Canada. A Newfoundland named Tang was credited with saving 92 people aboard the ship by bringing the *S.S. Ethie* to shore.

BUILT FOR WATER RESCUE

Newfoundlands's bodies are specially designed for work in the water. The dogs are large and muscular. They can weigh as much as 150 lbs. (68.04 kg) and stand as tall as 29 inches (73.7 cm) at the shoulders. Their size and strength make them perfect for towing people or boats through the water.

Newfoundlands have two coats of fur, which keep the dogs warm in frigid waters. The fur is oily, which allows it to repel water so that the dog's skin stays dry.

Newfoundlands have special physical characteristics, such as oily fur and muscular tails, that make them superb water rescue dogs.

The dog has a muscular tail that it uses to change directions while swimming. The breed's ears droop downward and its eyes are small and deep-set, which keeps water from entering the ears and eyes. A Newfoundland's loose upper lip creates a tight seal around anything the dog holds in its mouth. This seal allows the dog to carry items and swim without excess water entering its mouth and interfering with breathing. In addition, the dog's webbed feet make swimming easier. Interestingly, a Newfoundland does not doggy paddle when it swims; instead, the dog perfoms a broad breaststroke.

In 1919, a Newfoundland named Tang was working on a ship called the *S.S. Ethie*. The ship became caught on rocks off the coast of Canada. Tang jumped into the ocean and took the ship's rope in his mouth. With powerful strokes, he swam the entire ship to shore. Tang is credited with saving the 92 people aboard the ship. Tang was later presented with a medal for his bravery.

NEWFOUNDLANDS TO THE RESCUE

In some European countries, Newfoundlands are still used today to help drowning victims or swimmers caught in the ocean currents. With their human lifeguard counterparts, Newfoundlands stroll the beaches and keep a lookout for swimmers or boaters in danger.

Even though Newfoundlands are infrequently used as water rescue dogs in the United States, the Newfoundland Club of America encourages handlers and their dogs to participate in water rescue trials. These trials test the breed's water rescue abilities and keep the skills sharp.

Ana M. Ayala Hubbard is the owner of Amorosa Newfoundlands in Clinton Corners, New York. Hubbard has two Newfoundlands, Gypsie and Oslo. Both dogs have earned senior water rescue titles, one of the top categories of rescue titles offered by the Newfoundland Club of America.

How does Hubbard choose a puppy that might have the potential to succeed at water trials? Naturally, she needs to find a puppy that loves the water. "I like to see which puppy enjoys dunking his entire face and head when drinking from a water bucket," Hubbard says. She also wants a puppy that will go after a toy and return it to her. Retrieving skills are a must for water rescue because the dog is asked to bring items, people, and even boats back to shore.

Lauri Francis's Newfoundland, Domino Dodger, has earned his senior division water rescue dog title with his human handler's help.

Lauri Francis, the Web editor for the Genesee Region Newfoundland Club in New York, owns a 6-year-old Landseer Newfoundland named Domino Dodger. A Landseer Newfoundland has a distinctive black-and-white coat. The big dog has earned his senior division water rescue dog title. When picking a pup for water rescue work, Francis visits breeders who produce healthy and athletic dogs.

After the puppies are chosen, it is time to begin training the dogs for their lifesaving duties. Many days of challenging swimming and splashing lay ahead for both dog and handler.

Training to Save Lives

It required years of daily training before Hubbard's Newfoundlands, Gypsie and Oslo, and Francis's Domino Dodger earned their senior division water rescue dog titles. The learning began when the Newfoundlands were just pups.

In early puppy training, Hubbard teaches the dog obedience commands, like "sit," "stay," and "come." A water rescue Newfoundland especially needs to learn to retrieve things, like boat paddles and people, so the commands "pick it up" and "give" are important.

Domino Dodger learns how to grab a towline and haul a boat to shore. This life-saving technique gives the dog excellent experience in helping stranded boaters.

Hubbard will have to direct her dogs toward objects in the water, so the dogs learn directional commands, such as "left," "right," and "go out," which means to move away from the handler.

During water rescue work, Newfoundlands must be comfortable taking things, like a person's arm or towline, in their mouths. To teach the dog to accept an object in its mouth, Hubbard opens its mouth and places an item inside. She then removes it and gives the dog a treat as a reward. Next, Hubbard

WATER RESCUE TRIALS

The Newfoundland Club of America offers Newfoundlands and their handlers the opportunity to participate in three levels of water rescue trials. They are called junior division, senior division, and water rescue dog excellent.

The dog that successfully completes the junior division water trial is given a water dog (WD) title. These dogs have many requirements to complete, such as retrieving a floating bumper that's thrown 30 feet into the water, retrieving a life jacket that's dropped 50 feet (15.2m) from shore, and towing the boat, located 50 feet (15.2 m) away in the water, to the beach.

People play a vital part in helping the dog earn this title. Someone who is in the water 50 feet away from the beach pretends to drown. To successfully complete this task, the dog carries a line to the "drowning" victim. The dog also has to show endurance alongside its handler. The canine and its human partner have to swim side by side for 20 feet (6 m).

The more advanced senior division test awards the sucessful Newfoundland with a water rescue dog (WRD) title. For this title, the dog has to retrieve a life jacket and boat cushion that are dropped in the water 50 feet from the shore. Next, a helper rows a boat, taking the handler and dog, out onto the water. The canine must then jump from the boat and retrieve a lost paddle.

To demonstrate the ability to rescue drowning victims, the dog must bring a "drowning" helper, who is 75 feet (22.9 m) from the beach, a line and tow her to shore. Next, the dog retrieves an item from under the water. Then, the dog carries a line from the shore to a boat 75 feet (22.9 m) out in the water and hauls the boat back to the beach.

The most challenging trial, called the water rescue dog excellent, has even more demanding tasks. First, the dog must rescue two people who are holding onto the side of a boat, which is 75 feet

(continues)

(continued)

(22.9 m) from shore. As the Newfoundland reaches the stranded people, they hold onto the dog, and it swims with them to the beach. The next two tasks require the dog to tow a boat back to shore. A person pretends to be an unconscious drowning victim 75 feet (22.9 m) from the beach. The dog must swim to the person, grab her arm or life jacket, and bring her to safety.

To demonstrate top ability, the handler and dog are in a boat on the water. Three people pretend to be drowning, and the dog must jump from the boat to bring each "victim" back to the boat.

For the dog's final test, the Newfoundland watches a person in an inflatable boat capsize. The dog must swim 75 feet (22.9 m) to the victim, who is underneath the capsized boat, and bring her to shallow water. The dog can tow the person by the arm or the person can hold onto the dog.

Newfoundland dogs that exhibit these top-notch water-rescue skills can be lifesavers to people who are drowning, caught in a strong current, or stranded in a boat.

teaches the dog to hold the item on command. She puts something in the dog's mouth, applies gentle pressure to the top and bottom jaw, and commands, "hold." Gradually, she increases the amount of time the dog must keep the object in its mouth.

With the obedience and directional commands mastered, the Newfoundland is ready for water training. When the pup is between six and seven months old, Francis starts teaching it to retrieve lightweight items in the shallow water. She doesn't allow the dog to carry anything that is too heavy for it to handle. At 8 months old, she trains it to pull a small rubber raft. As the dog becomes older and its muscles become more mature, Francis lets it retrieve and tow increasingly heavier items.

To build the dog's swimming skills and endurance, Francis takes the Newfoundland to an area lake, and they swim side by side. She teaches the dog how to jump off docks, so it will be comfortable leaping into the water for the rescue trials.

Lauri Francis and Domino Dodger practice water rescue techniques with other Newfoundlands and their handlers. Here, the pair takes a break from water rescue trials.

For advanced training, Francis enlists a group of helpers to practice each activity that will be tested during water trials. She needs people who can pretend to be in distress in the water, so the dog can learn to rescue them. The Newfoundland is taught to bring the "drowning" individual a line. It learns to allow the person to grab its shoulders or hindquarters and swim the victim to shore. In addition, the dog is trained to pull an "unconscious" victim to safety by holding the victim's arm or life jacket.

During some exercises, the dog learns to jump from a boat to retrieve a paddle. At other times, the dog is commanded to swim out to the boat and tow it to shore. All told, these advanced training sessions can last up to three hours and usually occur three times a week.

Domino Dodger's rigorous practice sessions proved successful when he earned his senior division water rescue dog title. Of course, Lauri Francis is proud of her dog's water rescue skills, but what really amazes her about Newfoundlands is their unselfish nature. "They will put their lives on the line for somebody they don't even know," she says.

Protective Pets

Belle, a 17-pound beagle, is truly her handler Kevin Weaver's guardian angel. Weaver has **diabetes**, and Belle is a diabetic service dog. Diabetes is a chronic condition in which high levels of sugar are found in a person's blood. Belle periodically checks the amount of sugar in Weaver's body by licking his nostrils and sniffing his breath. If Belle detects a problem with Weaver's blood sugar, she whines and paws at Weaver's leg. Then, Weaver uses his diabetes monitor to test a small amount of his blood and take whatever medical action is needed.

Because Weaver has diabetes, it's important for him to frequently monitor his blood sugar levels. One day, Weaver's blood sugar dropped dangerously low. He had a seizure and became unconscious. Belle jumped into action and did what she had been trained to do in an emergency. She located Weaver's cellular telephone and bit down on the number 9, which had

Kevin Weaver is thankful for his dog Belle, who contacted emergency dispatchers when Weaver had a seizure and became unconscious. Without Belle's help, Weaver might not have been saved.

FLUFFY, THE HONORABLE WAR DOG

Sgt. 1st Class Russell Joyce was serving in the Special Forces in northern Iraq when his unit asked for a dog to help guard them. The Kurds offered Joyce's unit an Iraqi-born German shepherd that weighed only 36 pounds, had many scars, and was missing some teeth. Though the dog was being called Tera Kazez, Joyce renamed him Fluffy.

Joyce gained Fluffy's trust by caring for him and feeding him. Then, Joyce began training Fluffy as a guard dog, teaching the dog to respond to English commands.

After training, Fluffy served the Special Forces unit bravely. He kept

Thanks to Sgt. 1st Class Russell Joyce, Fluffy was flown to the United States to be reunited with Joyce and his family, after the canine and his military partner served in Iraq.

the soldiers safe by chasing and stopping intruders. He even worked beside the men as they fought to occupy a mountain north of Mosul.

In early May 2003, Joyce received his orders to return to the United States. He made certain that all of Fluffy's vaccinations were current so that the dog could go home with him. However, the military would not allow Fluffy to fly to the United States because he

(continues)

(continued)

wasn't an official military working dog. Joyce was forced to leave Fluffy behind.

As soon as Joyce arrived home, he began contacting people who could help bring Fluffy to the United States. Ron Aiello, president of the United States War Dogs Association, Inc., was especially helpful. Aiello was the handler of a military K-9 named Stormy during the Vietnam War. Because many military dogs were left in Vietnam following the War, Aiello understood the heartbreak Joyce felt.

Many Americans heard about Fluffy's plight and voiced support for the dog. Soon, the military responded and named Fluffy an honorary military working dog with honorary war dog status. At the end of May, Fluffy was flown to the United States to be reunited with his human family.

Fluffy is now retired from service and is living happily in Fort Bragg, North Carolina. Fluffy won the Extraordinary Service to Humanity Award, and the Iams Company awarded Fluffy with a lifetime supply of dog food. But the best reward for this brave canine is living the rest of his days surrounded by people who love him.

been programmed to call 9-1-1. The dispatcher who answered the call heard Belle barking and understood that help was needed.

Emergency personnel arrived in time to aid Weaver. The doctors were convinced that Belle had saved his life. They said that if Weaver had to wait for a human to summon help for him, he probably would have died.

Belle was the first dog ever to receive the VITA Wireless Samaritan Award, which is given to someone who uses a cell phone to save a life.

HUNTING FOR HELP

One winter's day, 36-year-old Michael Miller went quail hunting with Sadie, his English setter. They walked together across the backyard and toward the woods.

The pair was about one third of a mile from Miller's house, when the man had terrible chest pain and collapsed to the ground. He was having a heart attack. Miller used his hunting dog whistle to call Sadie to him. She came and stood by his side.

Miller was too weak to stand and walk. He grabbed hold of Sadie's collar. The 45-pound (20 kg), dog used all of her strength to drag Miller, who weighed 180 pounds (82 kg), the full distance back to the house. Once there, Sadie barked until Miller's wife came to the door and found them.

Miller's wife called for emergency help. Miller was rushed to the hospital and had triple bypass heart surgery. For Sadie's life-saving actions, the dog was awarded the 44th Reward Dog Hero of the Year award, sponsored by Heinz Pet Products.

LATER, ALLIGATOR

Eighty-three-year-old Ruth Gay took her Australian blue heeler, Blue, for an evening walk in her backyard. As the pair walked, Gay fell to the ground, breaking her nose and dislocating her shoulder.

Blue kept a close guard at Gay's side until, all of a sudden, he growled and darted away. Gay heard the sounds of the dog fighting with something, but she couldn't see what it was.

When Gay's daughter and son-in-law returned home, they discovered Gay and took her to the hospital for treatment. They also brought Blue to the veterinarian. Blue had suffered 30 cuts, the longest of which was a 3-inch (8 cm) gash in his stomach. The veterinarian said that Blue had fought an alligator and won.

Blue had managed to keep the alligator from attacking Gay as she lay injured and helpless on the ground. For his bravery, Blue was given the 2002 Del Monte Dog Hero Award.

6
Dogs in World War II

Dogs perform heroic feats in search and rescue, police work, and many other areas in which people need help. Some people might be surprised to know that dogs also serve in the military. In fact, military dogs have been loyal protectors of United States service members since World War II.

During the Second World War, brave canine heroes walked through the dense jungles of the Pacific, helping soldiers locate enemy attackers. The canines would silently warn their handlers when they detected the presence of the enemy. These scout dogs saved many lives with their alerts. Other dogs, trained as sentry canines, guarded U.S. beaches and military posts against enemy attacks and infiltration. Military sled dogs traveled through remote, icy regions to rescue crews from airplanes that went down.

Two dog lovers thought of the idea for the United States to use dogs during war. Arlene Erlanger, a well-respected dog breeder, and Arthur Kilbon, a fellow dog breeder and columnist for the *New York Sun,* joined forces in January of 1942 to begin the Dogs for Defense program.

Dogs for Defense asked the American people to donate dogs to be used by the military. At first, 30 different dog breeds were accepted for the program. The dog had to be between the ages of 14 months and 3 and a half years, 23–28 inches (58.4 cm–71.1 cm) in height, and 55–85 pounds (24.9 kg–38.6 kg). Later, the breeds that could be donated were narrowed to German shepherds, Doberman pinchers, Belgian sheepdogs, farm collies, giant schnauzers, Siberian huskies, malamutes, and Eskimo dogs.

On March 13, 1942, Dogs for Defense became the official agency for supplying and training military dogs for the Army Quartermaster Corps. In the summer of that year, the Quartermaster Corps took over the dog training duties. WWII military dogs were popularly known as the "K-9 Corps."

On June 13, 1942, soon after dog training began, a true threat to national security occurred. Four men disembarked from a German submarine and came ashore near Amagansett, Long Island, in New York. They carried explosives with the intent to attack. Another group of attackers entered the United States near Jacksonville, Florida. All men were captured before they caused any damage.

With these incidents fresh in the minds of military officials, the Coast Guard was provided with dogs trained as sentries to guard and protect people and property. These canines and their handlers guarded the Atlantic, Pacific, and Gulf coasts. All told, 3,174 sentry dogs were provided to the Coast Guard.

TRAINING THE WWII K-9

The Quartermaster Corps trained more than 10,000 dogs for the war. Whether the dog would eventually be a sentry, scout, or messenger K-9, all dogs began with basic training. The dogs were drilled in obedience. In wartime, a dog must repond quickly to commands for its own safety and the safety of its handler. The dogs learned to heel to the left side of the handler, opposite the handler's weapon arm. They were taught to lie down, to stay, and to come. The dogs responded to both verbal commands and hand signals because on the battlefield, spoken commands might give away the handler's position and put him in danger.

Military working dogs have been helping U.S. soldiers since World War II. War dogs of the past helped pave the way for today's military dogs, such as this K-9 who has been trained to search for illegal drugs and weapons. Here, the dog is searching for weapons in Baghdad, Iraq.

During initial training, the dogs needed to become accustomed to situations they would encounter in battle. They would need to stay focused on their jobs while gunshots sounded overhead and bombs exploded nearby. For this reason, the dogs were exposed to explosions and to rifle fire during training. The canines rode in various military vehicles so that they would be ready for any type of transport.

Part of each dog's preparation involved wearing a gas mask. The dog had to willingly wear the mask, which would protect it if chemical weapons were used. In battle, the dogs would be expected to cross rough terrain, so they had to be **agile**. They practiced crawling under low objects and jumping over high obstacles.

FOCUSING ON SPECIAL TASKS

After this beginning training stage, the dogs were taught their specialties. The majority of K-9s were trained as sentry dogs. Sentry training took eight weeks. The K-9s were trained to use their keen senses of smell and hearing to detect humans. The sentry dog would alert to an intruder with a growl or bark.

Sentry K-9s also learned to attack on command. To teach this skill, a person wore padding and played the part of an aggressor. The individual would pretend to threaten the dog with an item, such as a stick. The dog learned to attack when his handler gave the command. If the aggressor took out a gun, the dog was taught to bite his weapon arm.

Military scout dogs traveled with their handlers in front of the troops. This dog's job was to detect the presence of the enemy and alert its handler. Once trained, these amazing canines could detect an enemy from a distance of 1,000 yards (914.4 m).

Scout dog training required 12 weeks. Like the sentry dog, the scout dog learned to alert to human scent and sound. However, the scout K-9 was taught to give a silent alert by stiffening his body so that the enemy remained unaware of approach.

PRINCE OF THE ROYAL AIR FORCE

Michael Mouravieff-Apostol of Pleasant Valley, New York, recalled the story of his mother's dog, Prince, and Prince's WWII service with England's Royal Air Force.

Mary Hall-Caine, Mouravieff-Apostol's mother, lived in England when World War II began. The woman had a passion for dogs. Her 4-year-old German Shepherd, Prince, was a loyal companion and was trained to keep her safe.

Just like the U.S. Dogs for Defense, England had a program that asked citizens to volunteer their dogs for the war effort. Hall-Caine knew that Prince would make a wonderful dog for military service. He was intelligent, large, muscular, and highly trained. She made the difficult decision to donate her beloved Prince.

Prince became a guard dog at a Royal Air Force base. He and his military handler helped keep the base free of enemy intruders. Prince worked for the military from 1939 until 1945.

When his brave service ended, Prince was retrained for family life. His handler delivered him back to the Mary's door. She and her family were concerned that Prince might be aggressive around their toddler, Michael, but Prince proved to be a gentle playmate. Hall-Caine was proud of Prince's dedicated service to England. On her piano, she displayed the certificate of thanks for Prince's contribution, which the British government had provided to her. Today, that framed certificate has a place of honor in Mouravieff-Apostol's home.

K-9 Handler Staff Sgt. Allisa Jones waits for a helicopter lift with her explosion detection dog Marco, a Belgian Malinois who was deployed to Iraq with Jones from Tinker Air Force Base, Oklahoma.

The military also used messenger dogs during WWII. These K-9s carried messages in pouches on their collars. Each messenger dog had two handlers and made communication runs between them. The messenger dog's job was necessary to bring information from the front lines to the rear command post and vice versa. Sometimes the dogs raced 1000 yards (914.4 m) between handlers.

For messenger dog training, it was vital to establish a strong relationship between the canine and both handlers. The handlers took turns with feeding and training. At first, the dog learned to run a short trail between the handlers. Gradually, the distance the dog had to cover increased so that one of the handlers was out of the dog's line of sight. The dog would have to rely on its acute senses to locate each handler. As the training advanced, the terrain of the trails became more difficult. The K-9 would be called upon to cross streams and navigate wooded areas to deliver the important message.

With the training complete, the canines were ready to serve the country. Each dog would serve bravely, and a special few would be remembered for generations to come.

7
War Dog Heroes

Once given their wartime assignments, many WWII military dogs acted bravely and even heroically. One well-known K-9 hero, Chips, was a mix of German shepherd, collie, and Siberian husky. Edward J. Wren of Pleasantville, New York, donated the dog to Dogs for Defense. Chips was trained as a sentry dog.

Chips and his military handler, Army Private John Rowell, were involved in the invasion of the Italian island of Sicily in July 1943. Suddenly, Chips broke loose from Rowell and headed straight for a

FALA, THE FAMOUS SCOTT

Fala was a black Scottish terrier that belonged to President Franklin D. Roosevelt (FDR), the 32nd president of the United States. The terrier was popular among the American people. He received so many letters from admiring youngsters that a secretary was assigned to answer Fala's fan mail.

Fala was President Franklin D. Roosevelt's beloved Scottish terrier who accompanied the President on many historically important trips. Today, the pair is remembered at FDR's memorial in Washington, D.C.

President Roosevelt loved Fala, and the dog returned the affection by following him everywhere. FDR taught the Scotty a multitude of amusing tricks. Fala accompanied FDR on historic trips around the world. One of those famous trips occurred during a very important time in history. In August 1941, Fala was on the war ship near the coast of Newfoundland, where President Roosevelt and England's Prime Minister Winston Churchill created the Atlantic Charter.

After Roosevelt died on April 12, 1945, Fala continued to hope that his master would return. When General Dwight D. Eisenhower came to lay a wreath at FDR's grave, sirens accompanied his motorcade. Fala became excited, and Mrs. Roosevelt believed that Fala thought it was FDR coming home.

Fala died on April 5, 1952, and is buried close to his master in Hyde Park, New York. A bronze statue of Fala sits ever-faithful next to a likeness of FDR at the president's memorial in Washington, D.C.

camouflaged machine gun pillbox. He dove into the pillbox. Moments later, an Italian soldier emerged with Chips attacking him. Then, three more enemy soldiers surfaced and surrendered. In the midst of the fight, the K-9 received a scalp injury. Later that same night, Chips alerted his handler to ten more Italian soldiers, and Rowell took them prisoner. The U.S. military awarded Chips the Silver Star, its third highest medal for valor, as well as the Purple Heart for his heroic actions.

Word reached the United States that a K-9 had received the Purple Heart, a military decoration given to people who are wounded in combat. When William Thomas heard the news, he was concerned. Thomas was the former national commander of the Military Order of the Purple Heart, and he believed that the medal should be reserved for human heroes. He wrote to government officials, including President Franklin D. Roosevelt, to voice his objection. Major General J.A. Ulio ordered that Chip's medals be taken back.

Another heroic K-9, a German shepherd named Caesar, was trained as a messenger dog during World War II. He and his two handlers, Marine PFC Rufus Mayo and Marine PFC John Kleeman, were fighting in the Solomon Islands in early November 1943. Mayo and Caesar were in a foxhole. The dog leaped from the hole and alerted his handler to the presence of a Japanese soldier. Two bullets hit Caesar, but Mayo was able to shoot the soldier. The dog had saved Mayo's life.

Not all dogs from the United States could serve heroically during World War II, so the Dogs for Defense offered the canines and their handlers another way to contribute. A dog's owner could purchase the canine a military rank for a certain sum of money, which ranged from $1 to $100 depending on the level of rank desired. The program raised $75,000 for the war effort. Even President Franklin D. Roosevelt bought the rank of private for his Scottish terrier, Fala.

At the end of the war, most military K-9s were returned to their owners. Before their homecomings, the dogs were retrained to be family pets. They were exposed to hours of friendly human contact to teach them to trust people and not to act aggressively. In a final test, a trainer jumped out from behind a building or bush, waving a stick. If the dog greeted him without aggression, the canine was ready for family life.

Military Canines Today

Military dogs continue to make vital contributions to the United States Armed Forces, both on the home front and abroad. During the Korean War, about 1,500 K-9s served the United States. Brave canines were relied upon once again during the Vietnam War.

Sentry dogs and their handlers were used to guard military bases throughout the Vietnam War. On December 4, 1966, Tan Son Nhut Air Base—a combined base of U.S. and South Vietnamese forces—

was attacked. Three sentry dogs and one handler were killed.

A2C Robert Thorneburg and his German shepherd dog, Nemo, were on patrol. Nemo alerted his handler to the enemy, and Thorneburg released him. The K-9 was shot in the eye. Thorneburg was able to kill one of the **Vietcong** fighters, but Thorneburg was wounded.

Even though Nemo was seriously injured, he crawled on top of Thorneburg to shield him until help arrived. Both Nemo and his handler were rescued, but Nemo never regained sight in his eye.

Enemy Vietcong fighters were specialists in **guerilla warfare**. They knew how to use the natural environment to their advantage. The soldiers would hide in the jungle to stage a surprise strike. Scout dogs were used to detect the hidden enemy before they could attack. The scout K-9 and handler walked in front of the troops, and the dog would silently alert if he sensed the Vietcong.

The Vietcong built a complex system of underground tunnels, where they could plan and launch military attacks. They also dug holes called punji pits. Inside the holes, the Vietcong placed upright sharpened stakes covered with manure. The pit was camouflaged so the American soldiers didn't know its location until it was too late. If the soldier wasn't killed by his fall on the stakes, his wound became infected because of the germ-laden feces.

To defend against these tactics, the U.S. military trained tunnel K-9s. The dogs were taught to use their keen sense of smell to find the tunnels and punji pits. They learned to alert by sitting about 2 feet (.6 m) from the tunnel entrance or pit.

German shepherds, like Quasar above, and Belgian Malinois go through a series of agility and aggression training before entering service as military working dogs. Army Sgt. Carlos Cruz works with Quasar to properly train the dog for demanding military work.

The Vietcong also set explosive booby traps. The United States trained mine dogs to locate these explosives with their keen noses. Like tunnel dogs, the mine K-9s were taught to sit a small distance from the devices to alert their handlers.

Sadly, after their brave service, most of the Vietnam War canine veterans were left behind in that country. They were considered merely military equipment. There was no widespread program, as existed after WWII, to reintroduce the dogs to U.S. civilian life.

CURRENT TRAINING

Today, the responsibility of obtaining and training military dogs lies with the 341st Training Squadron at Lackland Air Force Base in Texas. The dog breeds used for standard military working dogs are the German shepherds and Belgian Malinois.

These breeds have desirable physical traits that make them well suited to military work. They have a double coat of fur that allows them to adapt to either hot or cold climates. In addition, the dogs have an exceptional sense of smell and are strong and fast. German shepherds and Belgian Malinois also have personality traits that make them easy to train. These dogs are intelligent and willing to work. They also display confidence and courage, necessary traits for the daily demands of the military.

Nine-week-old Falcor relaxes with military working dog trainer Staff Sgt. David Adcox. Many military pups are purchased from well-respected breeders, but Falcor is part of the puppy program, a military working dog breeding program at Lackland Air Force Base.

The 341st Training Squadron purchases their dogs from well-respected breeders. In 1998, the squadron also began a breeding program of its own, which produces both German shepherds and Belgian Malinois. To be certain the dogs have the proper personality and are in good health, they undergo stringent temperament and physical evaluations. Before they are chosen for military dog training, they are evaluated for **assertiveness**, **temperament,** and intelligence.

If the tests indicate that the dogs would not perform well as military K-9s, they are placed elsewhere. They may be used to train handlers, utilized in the breeding program, or given to another government

A MILITARY DOG'S RETIREMENT

After the Vietnam War, dogs that heroically served and saved human lives were left behind in the country. The dogs were considered military equipment and were abandoned by the U.S. military. A law passed in 2000 made certain that military working dogs would no longer be considered military equipment. The law paved the way for the dogs to go elsewhere when their service in the military was complete.

Now, military dogs that are still able to work can be acquired by other government law enforcement agencies. On the other hand, if the dog is ready to enjoy retirement, his military handler is given the option of taking the K-9 home with him. If the handler cannot adopt the dog, another caring family can welcome the canine into their home. They will make sure the dog is comfortable in its well-deserved retirement.

Marine Lance Cpl. John Paul Schilling and his military working dog, Bosco, search for weapons in Iraq on December 5, 2005. Military working dogs work hard to help keep soldiers and civilians safe during times of war.

agency. The dogs might even become someone's beloved pet.

PROTECT AND PATROL

Most modern military canines are trained in patrol work. Like sentry dogs of the past, patrol K-9s partner with their handlers to guard. Military working-dog training requires approximately 15 weeks. At first, the handler and dog must form a close bond.

The handler spends many hours feeding, grooming, exercising, and playing with the dog.

During the next step, the dog undergoes obedience training, both on and off the leash. When confronted with danger, a military dog must respond to all commands without hesitation. All military dog training is done using a system of reward and punishment. If the canine performs the task correctly, it is rewarded with praise, petting, play, or food. On the other hand, if the dog needs correction, it receives a jerk on the leash.

An item that has been handled by a person will hold the individual's scent, which the dogs can then detect. Military patrol dogs are taught to detect human scents with their sensitive noses. The dogs learn how to find a person hiding in a building, as well as how to search for articles, such as weapons or backpacks.

Patrol dogs must learn to act aggressively. They are taught to attack a trainer, who wears padded clothing, on command. Patrol dogs are also trained to attack without a command whenever its handler is in physical danger.

The military working dog is a dual-purpose K-9. The dog is trained in both partol and detection work. Some patrol dogs will learn to detect illegal drugs such as marijuana, cocaine, and heroin. Other patrol canines will be taught to detect explosives. Once trained, these brave dogs work across the country and around the world, keeping U.S. armed service members safe.

Military working dogs join the ranks of other distinguished dogs that tirelessly use their intelligence and training to help others. Dogs like these deserve special recognition and have earned a respected place in canine history.

Glossary

Agile quick and graceful; limber

Assertiveness the ability to show strength and force

Antitoxin a substance, or serum, that is used to eliminate infection

Diabetes a chronic condition in which high levels of sugar build up in a person's blood

Diphtheria a disease caused by bacteria. Symptoms include a sore throat, swollen glands, fever, and weakness

Guerilla warfare the use of unconventional tactics, such as sabotage, to fight

Musher dogsled driver

Serum a liquid that can contain antibodies and is used to prevent or cure a disease

Temperament mental or emotional traits

Vietcong Communist forces fighting the South Vietnamese government

Bibliography

Blake, Robert J. *Togo.* New York: Philomel Books, 2002.

Born, K. M. "Quartermaster Dog Program." U.S. Quartermaster Foundation. Available online. URL: http://www.qmfound.com/K-9.htm

"Brave English Setter Named 44th Reward Dog Hero of the Year." dogandkennel.com. Available online. URL: www.petpublishing.com/dogken/news/heinz01.shtml.

Davis, Kathy Diamond. "Water Rescue Dog Tests For Newfoundlands." Available online. URL: VeterinaryPartner.com. 2005.

Dean, Charles L. *Soldiers and Sled Dogs: A History of Military Mushing.* Lincoln, Nebraska: University of Nebraska Press, 2005.

Derr, Mark. *A Dog's History of America.* New York: North Point Press, 2004.

"Diphtheria." Mayo Clinic. Available online. URL: http://www.mayoclinic.com/health/diphtheria/DS00495

"Fala." Franklin D. Roosevelt Presidential Library and Museum. Available online. URL: http://www.fdrlibrary.marist.edu/falabio.html

Francis, Lauri (Genesee Region Newfoundland Club, Webmaster, Newfoundland Handler), Telephone interview with the author. October 7, 2005.

"Gator-Fighting Dog is 'Dog Hero of the Year'" *The Scoop.* April 5, 2002. Dogs in the news.com. Available online. URL: http://dogsinthenews.com/issues/0204/articles/020405a.htm

Gorrell, Gena K. *Working Like a Dog*. Toronto, Ontario: Tundra, 2003.

"History of the Port Authority." Port Authority Police Department of New York and New Jersey. Available online. URL: http://www.panynj.gov/

Hubbard, Ana M. Ayala (Amorosa Newfoundlands, Owner, Breeder, and Handler). E-mail interview with the author, September 28, 2005.

"In Loving Memory of Sirius." Available online. URL: http://our.homewithgod.com/mkcathy/sirius.html

Jackson, Donna M. *Hero Dogs: Courageous Canines in Action*. New York: Megan Tingley Books, 2000.

"K-9 Unit." Port Authority Police Department of New York and New Jersey. Available online. URL: http://panynj.gov/

Krause, Louise (Author of *Heroes All Without Question*). Interview with the author, Cape May, New Jersey, July 20, 2005.

Lemish, Michael G. *War Dogs: A History of Loyalty and Heroism*. Washington, DC: Brassey's, 1999.

Lim, David W. (Port Authority Police Department of New York and New Jersey, Sgt. K-9 Trainer and Handler). Telephone interview with the author. May 4, 2005.

"Military Working Dogs." United States Air Force Fact Sheet, June 2005.

Miller, Debbie S. *The Great Serum Race: Blazing the Iditarod Trail*. New York: Walker and Company, 2002.

Mott, Maryann. "Dogs of War: Inside the U.S. Military Canine Corps." *National Geographic News.* April 9, 2003. Available online. URL: http://news.nationalgeographic.com/news/2003/04/0409_030409_militarydogs.html

———."Guard Dogs: Newfoundlands' Lifesaving Past, Present." *National Geographic News.* February 7, 2003. Available online. URL: http://news.nationalgeographic.com/news/2003/02/0207_030207_newfies.html

Mouravieff-Apostol, Michael (Owner of Prince K-9 for the Royal Air Force). Telephone interview with the author. November 17, 2005.

Newfoundland Club of America. Available online. URL: http://www.newfdogclub.org

"Police K-9 Sirius." Port Authority Police Memorial. Available online. URL: http://www.portauthoritypolicememorial.org/sirius.htm

Presnall, Judith Janda. *Rescue Dogs.* San Diego, CA: Kidhaven Press, 2003.

Rondeau, Adam (37th Training Wing Lackland Air Force Base Office of Public Affairs, 1st Lt.). E-mail interview with the author, November 18, 2005.

Salisbury, Gay and Laney Salisbury. *The Cruelest Miles: The Heroic Story of Dogs and Men in a Race Against an Epidemic.* New York: W.W. Norton & Company, 2003.

Smith, Leef. "A Bite and Bark That Saved a Life." *The Washington Post.* June 19, 2006. Available online.

URL: http://www.washintonpost.com/wpdyn/content/article/2006/06/18/AR2006061800857.html

"Statement of David Lim to the National Commission on Terrorist Attacks Upon the United States March 31, 2003." 9-11 Commission. Available online. URL: http://www.9-11commision.gov/hearings/hearing1/witness_lim.htm

"WTC Police Dog Remembered." CBS News. April 24, 2002. Available online. URL: http://www.cbsnews.com/stories/2002/04/24/terror/main507066.shtml

For More Information

Find out more about the training and work of the dogs in this book by contacting these organizations.

Amorosa Newfoundlands
www.amorosanewfoundlands.com
amorosanewf@aol.com

Franklin D. Roosevelt Presidential Library and Museum
4079 Albany Post Road
Hyde Park, New York 12538
1-800-FDR-VISIT
www.fdrlibrary.marist.edu

Genesee Region Newfoundland Club
www.grnewfdogclub.org

The Newfoundland Club of America
www.newfdogclub.org
info@newfdogclub.org

Office of Public Affairs
37th Training Wing
Lackland Air Force Base, Texas 78236-5157
210-671-2907
www.lackland.af.mil/

Port Authority of New York and New Jersey
225 Park Ave. South
New York, New York 10003
212-435-7000
www.panynj.gov

Quartermaster Museum OQMG
USA Quartermaster Center
1202 22nd Street
Fort Lee, VA 23801-1601
804-734-4203
www.qmmuseum.lee.army.mil/

George, Charles and Linda George. *Bomb Detection Dogs.* Mankato, MN: Capstone Press, 1998.

———. *Search and Rescue Dogs.* New York: River Front Books, 1998.

Gorrell, Gena K. *Working Like a Dog.* Toronto, Ontario: Tundra, 2003.

Jackson, Donna M. *Hero Dogs: Courageous Canines in Action.* New York: Megan Tingley Books, 2000.

McDaniel, Melissa. *Disaster Search Dogs.* New York: Bearport Publishing Company, Inc., 2005.

Miller, Debbie S. *The Great Serum Race: Blazing the Iditarod Trail.* New York: Walker and Company, 2002.

Presnall, Judith Janda. *Police Dogs.* San Diego, CA: Kidhaven Press, 2002.

———. *Rescue Dogs.* San Diego, CA: Kidhaven Press, 2003.

Ruffin, Frances E. *Police Dogs.* New York: Bearport Publishing Company, Inc., 2005.

West, Nancy. *Chips: The War Dog.* Thornwood, New Jersey: Hero Dog Publications, 2004.

Wilcox, Charlotte. *The Newfoundland.* Mankato, MN: Capstone Press, 2000.

Web Sites

Bureau of Alcohol, Tobacco, Firearms and Explosives

www.atf.gov/kids/canines.htm

Description of the training and work of the ATF explosives and narcotics detection K-9s

Central Intelligence Agency
www.odci.gov/cia/ciakids/dogs/index.shtml
Learn about the training and work of the CIA K-9s

Dog Owner's Guide Online Magazine
www.canismajor.com/dog/newf.html
Find out about Newfoundlands

Federal Bureau of Investigation
www.fbi.gov/kids/dogs/doghome.htm
Information about FBI K-9s

Federal Emergency Management Agency
www.fema.gov/kids/games/heroes
Pictures of FEMA urban search and rescue canines

The Official Site of the Iditarod Trail Sled Dog Race
www.iditarod.com/learn/history.html
Recounts the history of the serum run

The Official Fluffy Website: Fluffy's Journey
http://www.k9fluffy.com/
Read Fluffy's story and how his human family is helping others

U.S. War Dog Memorial Fund
http://uswardogs.org/id3.html
Learn about the canines that serve in the U.S. military

Picture Credits

Page:

5: AP Images/Mary Altaffer

7: Jeff Christensen/Reuters/ Landov

8: AP Images/Mike Derer

14: AlaskaStock

17: Bettmann/Corbis

19: Elias H. Debbas II

22: Tyrrell Mendis, The Impressionists

23: Peter Baxter

25: Courtesy of the Genesee Region Newfoundland Club

28: Courtesy of the Genesee Region Newfoundland Club

31: Courtesy of the Genesee Region Newfoundland Club

34: Courtesy of Kevin Weaver

35: U.S. Air Force photo by Staff Sgt. Jeffrey A. Wolfe

42: Department of Defense photo by Spc. Daniel T. Dark, United States Army

45: U.S. Air Force photo by Master Sgt. Scott Wagers

48: Wendy Kaveney Photography

53: U.S. Air Force Photos/Robbin Creswell

55: U.S. Air Force Photos/Robbin Creswell

57: Department of Defense photo by Lance Cpl. Mark E. Morrow, United States Marine Corps

Cover: © AP Images. Kevin Weaver and his diabetic service dog, Belle, accept the VITA Wireless Samaritan Award.

Index